Rainy Day

Pam Scheunemann

Consulting Editor, Diane Craig, M.A./Reading Specialist

Published by ABDO Publishing Company, 4940 Viking Drive, Edina, Minnesota 55435.

Printed in the United States.

Credits
Edited by: Pam Price
Curriculum Coordinator: Nancy Tuminelly
Cover and Interior Design and Production: Mighty Media
Photo Credits: AbleStock, Digital Vision, Photodisc, Stockbyte

Library of Congress Cataloging-in-Publication Data

Scheunemann, Pam, 1955-
     Rainy day / Pam Scheunemann.
          p. cm. -- (First words)
     Includes index.
     ISBN 1-59679-410-0 (hardcover)
     ISBN 1-59679-411-9 (paperback)
     1. Vocabulary--Juvenile literature. I. Title. II. First words (ABDO Publishing Company)
PE1449.S32745 2005
428.1--dc22
                                                                                        2005042939

SandCastle™ books are created by a professional team of educators, reading specialists, and content developers around five essential components that include phonemic awareness, phonics, vocabulary, text comprehension, and fluency. All books are written, reviewed, and leveled for guided reading, early intervention reading, and Accelerated Reader® programs and designed for use in shared, guided, and independent reading and writing activities to support a balanced approach to literacy instruction.

Let Us Know

After reading the book, SandCastle would like you to tell us your stories about reading. What is your favorite page? Was there something hard that you needed help with? Share the ups and downs of learning to read. We want to hear from you! To get posted on the ABDO Publishing Company Web site, send us e-mail at:

sandcastle@abdopub.com

SandCastle Level: Beginning

About This Series

The *First Words* series provides emerging readers with multiple opportunities to practice reading high-frequency words used in simple text. These books are appropriate for independent, shared, and guided reading.

Red Rebus Section (pages 4–11) Each spread features a predictable, repetitive rebus sentence with a familiar picture clue placed opposite a full-page photograph that strongly supports the text.

Blue Story Section (pages 12–17) An illustrated short story containing the featured sight words offers contextual, repetitive reading opportunities using simple text and familiar letter-sound correspondence.

Green Game Section (pages 18–21) A fun, read-together guessing game based upon the contents of the book expands vocabulary and increases comprehension.

Rebus Glossary (page 22) This list pairs the words and picture clues featured in the rebus sentences.

SandCastle First Thirty Sight Words List (page 23) Use this list to build phonics and word recognition strategies for emerging and beginning readers.

Sight Word Focus

a	am	at	can	comes	here
I	in	is	it	like	little
look	said	see	the	we	you

"I am in the !"
said Wendy.

"We like the !"
said Rita.

"Can you see the ?" said Andy.

"We like it in the ☀," said Amy.

Rainy Day

"I like it in the sun," said Ray.

Liz said, "Look at the clouds!"

16

"Here comes the rain!" said Ray.

It is a rainy day!

Look at me!

I am puffy.

I travel on the wind.

Rain comes from me.

What am I?